The First Step

By Michael Scotto
Illustrated By Evette Gabriel,
Dion Williams &
Joshua Perry

WELCOME TO MIDLaNDiA

OUR STORY BEGINS

Midlandia University

HERE

Community Center

Animal Land

Town Square

Playland Park

Bike Factory

Harvest Farms

STaRRiNG

HaRMONY
WaNNaDoGooD
The MusiciaN

Monday and Tuesday, Wednesday, Thursday, and Friday. Everyone in Midlandia worked hard all week.

But on the weekend, it was playtime! In the town square and beyond, the Midlandians played their favorite games and hobbies.

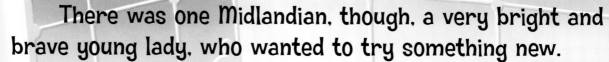

There was one Midlandian, though, a very bright and brave young lady, who wanted to try something new.

Harmony was a musician. She could play the drums and the banjo, the flute and the trombone. Today, she was in the mood to try a new instrument.

"I'm going to learn the clarinet!" she declared.

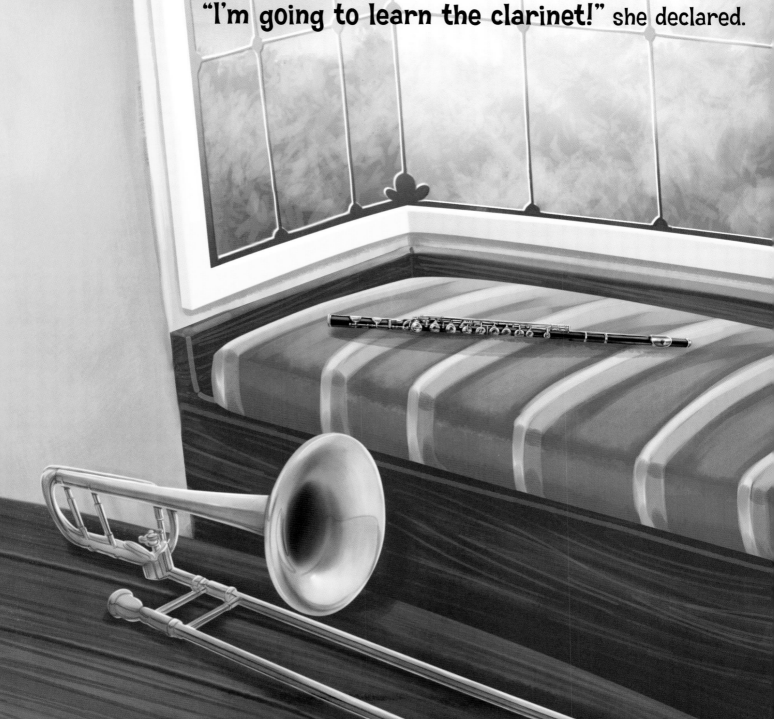

Harmony sat outside to practice. She imagined the beautiful songs she would play. "I'll sound prettier than a bird," she thought. When she blew her first note, though...

Harmony did not sound as pretty as a bird. Not even as good as a duck or goose. "I sound like a screaming monkey!" she cried. She took a deep breath and gave the clarinet another try. Instead of notes, all Harmony got were squeaks and squawks, and screeches and squeals. Others had started to notice.

"What is that terrible noise?" one Midlandian asked another.

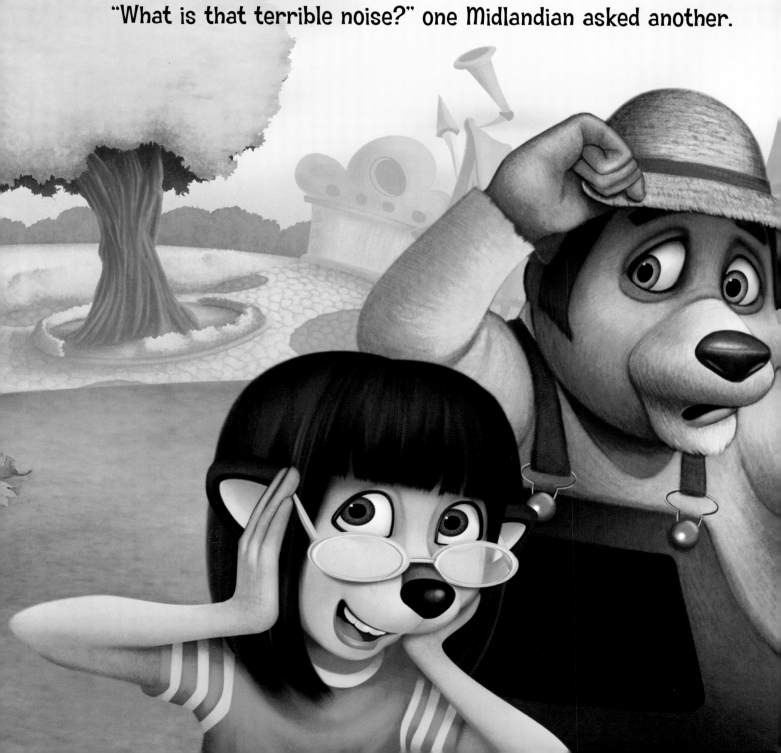

Soon, Chief Tatupu rushed around the corner where Harmony was playing. Chief was the leader of Midlandia. He was a great helper and friend.

"What is happening?" asked Chief. "I heard the most awful cries of pain!"

"Those weren't awful cries of pain!" Harmony moaned. "They were the awful cries of my clarinet."

Chief was very embarrassed. "Oh, I am sorry," he said. "I did not realize."

"I'm terrible at playing this thing," Harmony grumbled. **"I quit!"**

Chief knelt down beside Harmony. "You must not quit so soon," he said.

"Why not?" asked Harmony. "You said it yourself. I sound worse than a bicycle crash."

"I did not quite say that," Chief replied with a smile.
"If you want to know the truth, what you sounded like was
the first time Builda played tennis."

Harmony was puzzled. "That doesn't make any sense," she
said. "Builda is a great athlete, and tennis is her favorite hobby."

"She is very good at tennis now," replied Chief.
"But the first time Builda ever tried to play...

"She got all tangled up
and caused quite a racket."

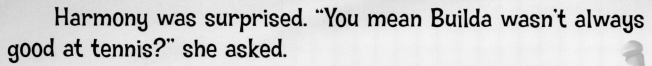

Harmony was surprised. "You mean Builda wasn't always good at tennis?" she asked.

"Almost no one does an activity very well the first time they try it," Chief said. He pointed around the town square.

"Look around," Chief said. "I bet that I could tell you a story about every single Midlandian out here."

Chief pointed at Doc Fixit. "Doc Fixit is the best doctor around," he said. "But the first time she put on someone's cast...

"She ended up in a very sticky situation."

"There is Sew, the seamstress," Chief noted. "She makes terrific dresses. But on her first try...

"Her work just did not measure up."

Chief spotted Bun, the town baker. "Bun makes delicious muffins every day," he told Harmony. "But I remember his first batch...

"It left him
quite battered."

"Posta delivers mail all around town on her bike," Chief said. "But the first time she tried to ride...

"She delivered herself right into the bushes."

Chief began to laugh. "And you should have seen me the first time I fished," he said. "On my first boat ride...

"Even you had a hard time with something new?" asked Harmony in amazement.

"Everyone does," Chief replied. "Trying a new thing is like walking on a long and bumpy journey. The first step is always the toughest one to take. You might be scared. You might even stumble. But without that first step, you can never go anywhere."

Harmony finally smiled. "You're right," she said. "I should get back to practicing. But maybe I'll take it inside, until I get a little better."

"Good luck!" Chief said.

Squeaking and squawking away, Harmony practiced her clarinet. It would be a long way off before she sounded as pretty as a bird.

But Harmony knew that bit by bit, and day by day, she would come closer by another step.

DISCUSSION QUESTIONS

Can you think of a new thing that you have tried recently?
Did you have fun? Do you think that you will try it again?

Harmony had a tough time playing the clarinet. If you were
Harmony's friend, what would you tell her to make her feel better?